엘리트 시선 67

숲속의 나무들
Trees in the Forest

장 현 경 시집
Jang Hyunkyung's poetry

엘리트출판사 Elite Publisher

나무들의 이야기

숲속의 나무들

장현경 시집

- 서문(序文)

아름다운 나무들의 이야기 1

　사람은 자연과 깊은 교감을 통해 삶의 지혜를 얻는다. 산책길을 따라 숲 속을 거닐다 보면, 살아 숨 쉬는 나무들의 생명체를 보게 된다. 그림 같은 나무들이 시인을 통해 신비로운 세계로 독자들을 이끌어 간다. 깊은 산속에 묵묵히 서 있는 나무들을 새로운 시선으로 바라보며 정교한 구조와 나무들의 능력을 관찰하게 된다. 세월이 흘러 나무의 뿌리가 인간의 머리에 비유되어 사람을 닮아가고 있다. 환상적인 건축물과 맑은 공기는 기쁨을 줄 뿐만 아니라 나무의 인지능력은 인간에게 흥미를 제공하고 있다.

　인간이 대지 위에 몸을 맡기고 살아가듯이, 사계절을 맞으며 숲 속 깊은 곳에 자리 잡은 나무들은 여기저기 편안하게 힘찬 모습을 보여준다. 이따금 불어오는 세찬 바람은 뿌리를 튼튼히 하려는 듯 마음껏 이파리를 흔들어 펼치게 한다. 나무들은 서로 다툴 줄을 모르고 사이좋게 지낸다. 더 가짐과 덜 가짐보다 함께 누림을 서로 지켜보며 분수에 맞는 몸짓으로 세상을 우러른다. 눈꽃 피운 나목들도 하늘이 주는 대로 불평 없이 앙상한 겨울나무로 자리를 지킨다.

　광활한 숲속의 나무들을 보니 눈이 시원해지고 마음도 밝아지고 기분마저 좋아진다. 시인으로 움츠린 몸에 기지개를 켜며 사계절 지지 않는 나무들의 이야기를 소재로 여기 한 권의 영역 시집을 다듬는다. 나무들의 이야기가 이 어려운 시대를 견뎌내는 수많은 독자에게 위로와 희망, 감동이 되기를 바란다.

　늘 따뜻한 성원을 보내주신 가족과 이웃의 지지에 고마운 마음 전하며 청계문학 가족 여러분의 건승을 빕니다. 나의 시편들을 만나는 존경하는 독자님께 건강과 행복이 늘 함께하시기를 기원합니다.

2025년 6월 청계(淸溪) 서재(書齋)에서

자정(紫井) 장현경(張鉉景) 근정(謹呈)

- Preface

The Story of the Beautiful Trees 1

People gain wisdom in life through deep communication with nature. When walking along the path in the forest, you see the living, breathing life of trees. Picturesque trees lead readers into a mysterious world through the poet. You look at the trees standing silently in the deep mountains with new eyes and observe the elaborate structure and abilities of the trees. As time passes, the roots of the trees are likened to human heads and resemble people. Fantastic architecture and clean air not only bring joy, but the cognitive abilities of the trees provide interest to humans.

Just as humans live on the earth, trees nestled deep in the forest show their strength and comfort as they meet the four seasons. The occasional strong wind blows, shaking the leaves as if to strengthen the roots. The trees do not know how to fight with each other and live in harmony. Rather than having more or less, they watch each other enjoy each other's company and look up at the world with gestures appropriate to their station. The bare trees covered with snow also keep their place as bare winter trees without complaint, as the heavens give them.

Looking at the trees in the vast forest, my eyes are refreshed, my heart is brightened, and my mood is lifted. As a poet, I stretch my body, which has been hunched over, and I am refining this volume of poetry based on the stories of trees that do not change throughout the four seasons. I hope that the stories of trees will be a source of comfort, hope, and inspiration to countless readers who are enduring these difficult times.

I would like to express my gratitude for the support of my family and neighbors for their warm support and pray for all the health and happiness of Cheonggye Literature Family. I wish you all the best health and happiness to my respected readers who meet my testimonies.

In June 2025, at Cheonggye Seojae
Jajeong, Jang Hyunkyung Raising

- 서시(序詩)

주목나무

신령스럽다
태백산의 상징은
주목(朱木)나무다

고산 지역에서만
볼 수 있는 나무로
낮은 지역에서는
볼 수 없는 희귀종

수명이
'살아 천년, 죽어 천년'
나무로 알려져 있다

분홍색 철쭉과
회색의 주목나무가
그립다.

– Opening poem

Yew Tree

It's divine
The symbol of Taebaeksan Mountain is
It's a yew tree

Only in mountainous area
With a tree that can be seen
In low areas
Rare species that can not be seen

Life span
'Live a thousand years, die a thousand years'
kwoan as a tree.

Pink azaleas and
The gray yew tree
I miss you.

contents

□ 서문(序文): 아름다운 나무들의 이야기 1
(The Story of the Beautiful Trees 1) ··· *004*

□ 서시(序詩): 주목나무(Yew Tree) ··· *008*

제 1 부 바오바브나무

참나무(The Oak Tree) ··· *016*

바오바브나무(Baobab Tree) ··· *018*

털개회나무(Hairy Oak) ··· *020*

화살나무(Arrow Tree) ··· *022*

엄나무(Acorn) ··· *024*

복숭아나무(Peach Tree) ··· *026*

이팝나무(Poplar Tree) ··· *028*

박달나무(Birch Tree) ··· *030*

사계절과 기후

명자나무(The Zelkova Tree) ··· *034*

제너럴 셔먼나무(General Sherman Tree) ··· *038*

제*2*부 비파나무

모과나무(Quince Tree) ··· *042*

살구나무(Apricot Tree) ··· *044*

비타민 나무(Vitamin Tree) ··· *046*

산사나무(Hawthorn Tree) ··· *050*

감나무(Persimmon Tree) ··· *052*

두릅나무(Elm Tree) ··· *054*

소나무(Pine Tree) ··· *056*

싸리나무(Sagebrush Tree) ··· *058*

석류나무(Pomegranate Tree) ··· *060*

contents

비파나무(Loquat Tree) ··· *062*

제*3*부 회화나무

포도나무(Grapevine) ··· *066*

불꽃나무(Fire Tree) ··· *068*

오동나무(Paulownia Tree) ··· *070*

회화나무(Pagoda Tree) ··· *072*

자두나무(Plum Tree) ··· *074*

때죽나무(Bamboo tree) ··· *076*

구기자나무(Matrimony Vine) ··· *078*

포포나무(Popo Tree) ··· *080*

아그배나무(Agabae Tree) ··· *082*

사계절과 기후

대추나무(Jujube Tree) ··· *084*

제4부 안개나무

수양버들(Weeping Willow) ··· *090*

자귀나무(Acacia Tree) ··· *092*

은행나무(Ginkgo Tree) ··· *094*

안개나무(Fog Tree) ··· *098*

치자나무(Gardenia Tree) ··· *102*

체리나무(Cherry Tree) ··· *104*

감귤나무(Citrus Tree) ··· *106*

야자수나무(Palm Tree) ··· *108*

골담초나무(Corduroy Tree) ··· *110*

contents

편백나무(Cypress Tree) ··· 112

제5부 올리브나무

대나무(Mamboo Tree) ··· 116

올리브나무(Olive Tree) ··· 118

단풍나무(Maple Tree) ··· 120

산수유나무(A Cornelian Tree) ··· 124

국수나무(Noodle Tree) ··· 128

선비나무(Scholar Tree) ··· 130

동백나무(Camellia) ··· 132

모감주나무(Motherwort) ··· 136

자카란다 나무(Jacaranda Tree) ··· 138

후박나무(Mackerel) ··· 140

제 1 부

바오바브나무

5,000살이 넘도록
빗물만 먹었나!
모자람을 살리는 신비한 나무
굵은 줄기를 가진 거대한 나무

참나무

봄이 오면
세찬 비바람과
한겨울의 추위를
견뎌내고
꿋꿋하게 자란다

여름엔
반짝반짝 타오르는
황금빛 이파리

가을엔
모든 것을 훌훌 털어버리고
고고한 흔적을
보여준다

겨우내
단단한 열매
맨몸으로
온 산에 흩어 뿌린다.

The Oak Tree

When spring comes
Heavy rain and wind
The cold of midwinter
Rrow up strong

In summer
Sparkling and burning
Golden leaves

In the fall
Shake everything off
A noble trace
Show

All winter
Hard fruit
With naked body
Scattered all over the mountain.

바오바브나무

그대에게
행운을 가져다주는
6,000년 수령
불멸의 나무
생각나고 그립다

신(神)이 심은 나무
우산 모양의 화려한 자태
왕관 모양의 꽃

5,000살이 넘도록
빗물만 먹었나!

모자람을 살리는 신비한 나무
굵은 줄기를 가진 거대한 나무

아, 보고파라

바오바브나무의 환상적인 일몰
오늘도 잊지 않고 기억하리!

Baobab Tree

To you
Bringing good luck
6,000 years old
Tree of immortality
I miss you and think of you

The tree planted by God
A gorgeous umbrella-shaped figure
Crown shaped flower

For over 5,000 years
Did you only drink rainwater?

The Mysterious Tree That Saves the Poor
A huge tree with a thick trunk

Oh, I miss you

Fantastic sunset over the baobab trees
I will remember and not forget today!

털개회나무

우연히
숲속을 거닐다가
눈에 띈 털개회나무

초록 숲에
꽃이 활짝 피어

풍성한 자태와
순백의 향연이
지난 추억을 그린다

꽃길 따라
그 향기에 취해
고개를 갸우뚱

지나는 이의 발길을
멈추게 하네!

Hairy Oak

By chance
While walking in the forest
A striking hairy oak tree

In the green forest
The flowers are in full bloom

Rich appearance and
A feast of pure white
Draw past memories

Along the flower path
Intoxicated by the scent
Tilt your head

The footsteps of those passing by
Stop it!

화살나무

첫가을
화살나무 분홍 단풍이
아름다워
계절을 재촉한다

3m의 키에
화살깃처럼 보이는 대궁을
이파리와 열매가 에워싸고

이파리는 된장국을 끓여 먹고
차로 마시고

가지는 달여서 불면증에
열매는 혈액순환에
뿌리는 면역력 강화에 쓰여

화살나무가 준 선물
오래오래
건강을 지키자!

Arrow Tree

First autumn
Arrow tree pink maple leaves
Beautiful
Urge the season

At 3m tall
A longbow that looks like an arrow feather
Surrounded by leaves and fruits

Boil the leaves in soybean paste stew and eat them
Drink it with tea

Eggplants are used to treat insomnia
The fruit is good for blood circulation.
The roots are used to strengthen immunity.

A gift from the arrow tree
For a long time
Stay healthy!

엄나무

이 더위에 자라는 새싹들
탐스럽게 자라
앙증맞고 귀엽다

10년이 넘어야 꽃이 피고
별들이 꿀을 따러 오는
아름다운 자연

언 듯 보니
맛있는 열매를 자랑

거친 가시 몸집
대문에 걸어두면
온갖 피부병에
효과가 있네

노랗게 핀 엄나무꽃
귀신을 쫓는 꽃
이름과 달리 볼수록 예뻐
건강을 주는 나무
삶의 질을 높인다.

Acorn

Sprouts growing in this heat
Grow up nicely
Cute and adorable

It takes more than 10 years for the flower to bloom
The stars come to collect honey
Beautiful nature

At first glance
Boasting delicious fruit

Rough thorn body
If you hang it on the front door
For all kinds of skin diseases
It works

Yellow blooming magnolia flowers
Flower that exorcises ghosts
Unlike its name, it looks prettier the more you look at it
The tree that gives health
Improves quality of life.

복숭아나무

봄비가 내린 후
아지랑이 하늘거리는 봄날

바위틈에
진달래 피고
개나리 샛노랗다

감미로운 향기를 품은 매화
빛깔이 고운 이화
화사한 벚꽃과 살구꽃
멀리 있어도 눈에 잘 보이고

엷은 분홍빛 복사꽃
활짝 피어
바람에 미소 짓네!

밤나무 감나무…

언덕으로 달리는 봄
향기를 가득 담은 꽃의 바다에
잠시 머문다.

Peach Tree

After the spring rain
A spring day with azure skies

In the crevice of the rock
Azaleas are blooming
Forsythia is bright yellow

Plum blossoms with a sweet fragrance
Beautifully colored pear blossoms
Brilliant cherry blossoms and apricot blossoms
It is visible even from far away

Pale pink copy flower
In full bloom
Smile in the wind!

Oak tree, persimmon tree…

Spring running up the hill
In a sea of flowers filled with fragrance
Stay for a while.

이팝나무

이팝나무가

올 한 해
풍년 농사를 위해

초여름에
가로수 좌우로

하얗게 꽃을
수놓고 싶어 하네!

Poplar Tree

The poplar tree

All year long
For a good harvest

In early summer
On the left and right of the street trees

White flowers
I want to embroider!

박달나무

깊은 산기슭에
박달나무가 30m까지
곧게 자라 숨을 쉰다

돋아나는 싹이 봄을 반기고
마을의 신령수처럼
가지가 많이 퍼져
전체가 둥그스름하다

목질이 단단해
방망이 홍두깨 절구를 만들고

세상을 보려는 듯
산들바람에 향기를 흩날리며
활짝 핀 박달나무꽃
별처럼 은은히 빛나는구나

광야의 표범인 양
박달재 고개를 그리며
우리 민족을 대표하는
가장 오래된 나무

그 모진 나날을
기도하듯
세상을 향해 잠시 발걸음 멈추며
지켜보고 있네!

Birch Tree

Deep in the foothills
The birch tree grows up to 30m
Grow up straight and breathe

The sprouting buds welcome spring
Like the spirit tree of the village
The branches spread out a lot
The whole thing is round

The wood is hard
Make a bat, a hammer, and a pestle

As if trying to see the world
Spreading its fragrance in the breeze
Full bloomed poplar flowers
Shining softly like a star

A lamb like a leopard in the wilderness
Drawing the head of Park Dal-jae
Representing our people
The oldest tree

Those harsh days
As if praying
Taking a moment to pause towards the world
I'm watching you!

명자나무

봄이면
아련히 떠오르는 명자나무

움츠렸던 대지에
촉촉이 비 내리면
대자연이 부르는
생명의 부활, 명자나무

봄날의 빨간 설렘처럼

시샘을 하는지
사이가 좋은지
옹기종기 모여서
매혹적인 웃음 듬뿍 짓네!

집 담장 밖
거리의 울타리
어디에서나 볼 수 있는
아가씨 나무, 명자나무

무어라
얘기할 듯
망설이는 듯
얼굴 불그스레

나에게 사랑을
고백하려나 봐!

The Zelkova Tree

In spring
A faintly rising zelkova tree

On the shrunken earth
When it rains lightly
Mother Nature Calls
The Resurrection of Life, the Myungja Tree

Like the red excitement of a spring day

Are you jealous?
Are we on good terms?
Gathered together
What a charming smile!

Outside the house fence
Street fence
Can be seen anywhere
Miss tree, zelkova tree

What
I feel like talking
Hesitating
Face flushed

Love me
I guess he's going to confess!

제너럴 셔먼나무

캘리포니아
세쿼이아 국립공원에
위치한 이 나무는
지구상에서 가장 큰 나무

수령 약 2,200년에
85m의 키
아파트 25층 정도

가장 굵은 부분의
몸 둘레는 36m

최근 기후 변화로
인간이 딱정벌레와 싸워
나무를 치료해주고 있다

비슷한 나무가 많아
자연이 주는 아름다움을
제대로
느낄 수 있다.

General Sherman Tree

California
In Sequoia National Park
This tree is located
The largest tree on earth

It was built approximately 2,200 years ago.
85m tall
About 25th floor of an apartment

The thickest part
Body circumference is 36m

Due to recent climate change
Humans fight beetles
Treating the tree

There are many similar trees
The beauty that nature gives
Properly
I can feel it.

숲속의 나무들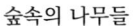

제 2부

비파나무

겨울에도 잎이 푸르고
비파를 닮은 듯한 열매
한 번 볼 때마다
젊어지네!

모과나무

봄에 피는 연분홍빛 꽃
앙증맞게 아름다워

수피에 흰무늬가
더욱 돋보이네

노랗게 잘 익은 모과
못생기긴 해도

차나 술 재료로 쓰이고

바구니에 담아
실내에 모아두면

은은한 향기 배어 나와
기분이 상쾌하고

한방에선
질병 치료제로 쓰이네!

Quince Tree

A light pink flower that blooms in spring
So cute and beautiful

White patterns on the skin
It stands out even more

Yellow ripe quince
Even though it's ugly

Used as an ingredient in tea and alcohol

Put in the basket
If you keep them indoors

A subtle fragrance spreads
I feel refreshed

In oriental medicine
It's used as a treatment for diseases!

살구나무

봄바람 살랑살랑
동구 밖 개울가에
외로이 서 있는 살구나무
한그루

진분홍 색깔로
발그무레하게 피워내는
살구꽃 마을

살구나무 가지마다
밤낮으로 아름답게
그리움을 터트리다가

세찬 비바람에
우수수 떨어지는 꽃바람으로

까마득한 지난날이
개울물과 졸졸 졸
스쳐 흘러가네!

Apricot Tree

Spring breeze blowing gently
By the stream outside the eastern district
Apricot tree standing alone
One tree

In a deep pink color
Blooming brightly
Apricot Blossom Village

On every apricot tree branch
Beautiful day and night
To burst out in longing

In the heavy rain and wind
With the wind blowing corn flowers

The distant past
Stream and trickle trickle
It just passes by!

비타민 나무

화려한 꽃과 향기를
지닌 비타민 나무
가던 발길을 멈추게 한다

2~6m의 키
수십 년의 수명
앙증스럽게 달려있는 열매

줄기는 가시가 많아
울타리로
주변 경관을 꾸미고

은백색의 이파리는
그늘을 만들어
시각적인 흥미를 유발한다

비타민 나무
꽃과 열매가
향기롭고 아름다워
사람에게 사랑을 받는다

비타민C가 풍부하여
차로
기침과 가래를 삭인다.

Vitamin Tree

Colorful flowers and fragrance
Vitamin tree
Makes one stop in one's tracks

Height between 2 and 6 meters
A lifespan of several decades
Fruit hanging gracefully

The stem has many thorns.
By the fence
Decorate the surrounding landscape

The silvery white leaves
Make a shade
Creates visual interest

Vitamin tree
Flowers and fruits
Fragrant and beautiful
Be loved by people

Rich in vitamin C
By tea
Relieves cough and phlegm.

산사나무

한낮에
햇빛을 모아
곱게 태운다
끝머리 하얀 꽃 유난히 곱다

자생지는 스칸디나비아
추운 곳에서 잘 자라

짙은 보랏빛 밤이 오면
물가에 뿌려진 산사나무꽃
노동절에 필요한 5월의 꽃

새벽녘
호숫가 산사나무 꽃송이에
간신히 걸린 그믐달

연못가에 산사나무꽃
배경 화면이 되어
그윽한 향기로
고즈넉이 피어있네!

Hawthorn Tree

At noon
Gather sunlight
Burn it nicely
The white flowers at the end are particularly pretty.

Native to Scandinavia
Grow well in cold places

When the deep purple night comes
Hawthorn blossoms scattered on the waterside
May Flowers for Labor Day

At dawn
In the flower buds of the hawthorn tree by the lakeside
The barely hanging moon

Hawthorn blossoms by the pond
Become a wallpaper
With a fragrant scent
It's blooming quietly!

감나무

라일락 향기 저무는 5월
골목마다 감꽃이
떨어질 때면
어릴 적 옛 동무가 생각난다

애틋한 마음
늘 곁에 있었지만
감꽃 목걸이
예쁘게 만들어
그대의 목에 걸어주지 못했다

쳐다보면 숨이 막혀
어쩌지 못하는 순간처럼
그렇게 떠나보내고

추억이 강물처럼 흐를 때
감꽃 향기 유난히 흩날리는
5월이 오면
오래오래 그리워했다.

Persimmon Tree

May, when the scent of lilac fades
There are persimmon flowers in every alley
When it falls
I remember my old friend from childhood

A heartfelt feeling
I was always by your side
Persimmon necklace
Make it pretty
I couldn't put it around your neck

When I look at it, it takes my breath away
Like a moment of helplessness
I sent it off like that

When memories flow like a river
The fragrance of persimmon flowers is particularly strong
When May comes
I've missed you for a long time.

두릅나무

사포닌과 비타민C가 풍부한 두릅은
봄나물의 제왕

입맛을 돋우고
면역력을 강화하고
피로를 해소하고
신장병을 예방하며
혈액순환과 혈당 저하에 도움이 되며

자연이 주는 식품으로
감기와 암 예방은 물론
피부 미용에 좋고
중풍 예방과 변비
위장 건강에 좋다

약간의 독성이 있는 두릅
데쳐 먹으면 된다.

Elm Tree

Elm, rich in saponin and vitamin C
King of spring vegetables

Whet your appetite
Strengthen your immune system
Relieve fatigue
Prevents kidney disease
It helps with blood circulation and lowering blood sugar levels.

With food provided by nature
Of course, it prevents colds and cancer.
Good for skin beauty
Stroke prevention and constipation
Good for stomach health

Slightly toxic elm
You can just boil it and eat it.

소나무

해마다
봄이 오면
꽃을 피우고 싶다

세기(世紀)마다 오는
소나무의 봄

오랜 세월
솔가지에 걸린
솔잎 향기에 취해

오래지 않아
기품 있게 머물던
그대의 세월에도

홍조 띤 고귀한 꽃을
보는 날이
드물지 않으리!

Pine Tree

Year after year
When spring comes
I want to bloom

Coming every century
Spring of the Pine Tree

For a long time
Hanging on a pine branch
Intoxicated by the scent of pine needles

Before long
Staying with dignity
Even in your years

A noble flower with a blush
The day I see you
It's not rare!

싸리나무

싸리나무 가지 꺾어
빗자루를 만들어

사각사각
마당을 쓸면
들리는 빗자루 소리

여름철
마당 구석에
누워있는 개를 보면
개 팔자가 그려진다

싸리나무 가지로
만든 작은 바구니
다래끼 광주리 삼태기 소쿠리…

한참 일하다가
해가 저물면
싸리문을 닫는다.

Sagebrush Tree

Break off a branch of a sagebrush tree
Make a broom

Square square
If you sweep the yard
The sound of a broom being heard

Summer season
In the corner of the yard
When you see a dog lying down
The dog's fortune is drawn

With a sagebrush branch
Small basket made
Daraeki Gwangjuri Samtaegi Sokuri…

After working for a while
When the sun sets
Close the sliding door.

석류나무

지울 수 없는
석류꽃의 원숙미(圓熟美)
가슴에 찍혀

그곳에서 헤어나지 못하던
까마득한 사춘기 시절

정겨움 가득했던
지난 세월의 뒤안길에서
달아오른 붉은 여성의 꽃

그 열매
황홀하여라

해마다 7월이면
그리운 듯
향기로운 꽃향기에 빠져
세월을 잊는다.

Pomegranate Tree

Indelible
The ripe beauty of pomegranate blossoms
Stamped on the chest

I couldn't get out of there
The distant days of adolescence

Full of affection
In the back alleys of years past
The flower of the red woman who is on fire

Lychee
Be ecstatic

Every year in July
I miss you
I fell in love with the fragrant scent of flowers
Forget the passage of time.

비파나무

5m의 키
푸근한 이파리
순백의 아름다운 꽃을

그윽한 마음으로
바라보는 사람들

열매와 뿌리 이파리가
한약재로 쓰일 때
수명이 연장되어
돋보이는 나무

겨울에도 잎이 푸르고
비파를 닮은 듯한 열매
한 번 볼 때마다
젊어지네!

Loquat Tree

5m tall
Warm leaves
Beautiful pure white flowers

With a deep heart
People looking at

Fruits and roots leaves
When used as a herbal medicine
Life is extended
A tree that stands out

The leaves are green even in winter
A fruit that resembles a loquat
Every time I see you
You're getting younger!

숲속의 나무들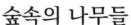

제3부

회화나무

임금이 하사하는
창덕궁 천년기념물 회화나무
금색으로 애절하게 망향의 꽃이 피었네

포도나무

포도꽃을 보자마자
대지의 푸름이 알알이 스며 있고
싱그러움이 한데 모여
송이송이 되어

갖가지 덩굴에 주렁주렁
뻗어 감는 넝쿨손 애틋하구나

둥글둥글 타원형 사이좋게
동글동글 줄줄이 함께하고

한알 두알 매혹적인 눈
여물고 여물어 향기로 감싸안아

검은 진주 눈물방울
포돗빛으로 반짝일 때

새콤달콤 진한 향기로
옹기종기 모여
누굴 기다리는지?

Grapevine

As soon as I saw the grape blossoms
The green of the earth is permeating every grain
The freshness gathers together
Become a songi songi

All kinds of vines hanging down
The vines that stretch out and wrap around me are so touching

Round and oval, nicely together
Round and round, together in a row

One grain, two grains, fascinating eyes
Wrapped in fragrance, wrapped in fragrance

Black Pearl Teardrop
When it sparkles like grapes

With a sweet and sour strong fragrance
Gathered together
Who are you waiting for?

불꽃나무

햇빛이 드는 가로수
봄에 심은
플레임 트리 구근이
싹을 틔워

꽃대가 살그머니 올라와
꽃잎처럼 생긴
작은 이파리가
빽빽하게
무리 지어

꽃송이가 피듯
발갛게 물들어
우리를 홀린다

마치 불길이 타오르듯
붉게
멋진 풍경을 만든다.

Fire Tree

Sunlit street trees
Planted in spring
Flame tree bulbs
Sprout

The flower stem is slowly rising
Shaped like a flower petal
A small leaf
Densely
In a crowd

As the flower buds bloom
Turn red
Bewitch us

As if a fire was burning
Red
It creates a beautiful landscape.

오동나무

오동나무는 가볍고 연하다

무늬가 아름답고
습기에 강하고
잘 뒤틀어지지 않아
악기를 낳는다

소리의 전달 성능도 좋아
가야금 거문고로 탄생한다

오동나무
천년이 지나도
가락을 잃지 않는다

한낮에도 환하게
꽃등을 켠
연보라색 오동나무꽃

딸을 낳으면
오동나무를 심어
같이 자란다.

Paulownia Tree

Paulownia is light and soft

The pattern is beautiful
Moisture resistant
It doesn't twist easily
Give birth to an instrument

The sound transmission performance is also good.
Born from the gayageum and geomungo

Paulownia tree
Even after a thousand years
Don't lose your tune

Bright even in broad daylight
Light the flower lamp
Purple paulownia flowers

If you have a daughter
Plant a paulownia tree
Growing up together.

회화나무

임금이 하사하는
창덕궁 천년기념물
회화나무

하늬바람 살랑살랑
생각나고 그립다

25m의 키
화려한 자태
고혈압의 예방과 치료

회화나무 금색으로
애절하게
망향의 꽃이 피었네

아, 보고파라

꽃과 이파리가
황금색이 되어
오늘도 잊지 않고
기억하리니!

Pagoda Tree

The wages are given
Changdeokgung Palace Millennium Monument
Pagoda tree

The gentle breeze blows
I miss you and think of you

25m의 키
Gorgeous appearance
Prevention and treatment of hypertension

In gold with the color of the pagoda tree
Desperately
The flower of longing has bloomed

Oh, I miss you

Flowers and leaves
Become golden
I won't forget today either
Remember!

자두나무

우리는 과수원에 세 들어 산다

자두나무 오얏나무 자도나무
이렇게 세쌍둥이는 순백의 꽃으로
호흡을 맞춰

4월에
아름다운 봄꽃으로
밀린 월세를 낸다

한여름 무더위에 땀을 뻘뻘
8월에는
빨갛게 익은 탐스러운 열매로
밀린 월세를 낸다

자두나무는
제날짜에 월세를 잘도 낸다.

Plum Tree

We live in an orchard

Plum tree, plum tree, plum tree
These triplets are like pure white flowers.
Get in sync

In April
With beautiful spring flowers
Pay the overdue rent

Sweating profusely in the midsummer heat
In August
With ripe, red, delicious fruit
Pay the overdue rent

The plum tree
He pays his rent on time.

때죽나무

사람들이
오가는 산책로에
때죽나무가 많아

검게 보이는 줄기는
항균
항염 진통제 역할을 하고

때죽나무껍질로
물고기를 기절시켜 잡고
빨래하여 때를 빼기도 한다

은은하고 달콤한 향기를
흩날리는 때죽나무꽃

멀리서도 울리는 종소리에
지나는 이의 발길을
멈추게 한다.

Bamboo tree

People
On the walking trail
There are a lot of bamboo trees

The stem that appears black
Antibacterial
It acts as an anti-inflammatory and analgesic.

With the bark of the bamboo tree
Catch a fish by stunning it
You can also wash it to remove stains.

A soft and sweet scent
Scattered azalea flowers

The sound of a bell ringing from afar
The footsteps of those passing by
Make it stop.

구기자나무

1년에 두 번 꽃이 피는
구기자나무

여름에 한 번 피며
열매 맺고
가을에 한 번 더 꽃이 핀다

뿌리껍질은 해열제로
줄기는 차(茶)로
어린잎은 나물이나 반찬으로
열매는 술을 만들고
말려서 불로장수하는 약재로 쓴다

하나 버릴 것 없는
구기자나무
봉사와 희생정신이 강해

함께 사랑하며
살아가려무나!

Matrimony Vine

Blooms twice a year
Matrimony vine

It blooms once in summer
Bearing fruit
It blooms once more in the fall

The root bark is an antipyretic
The stem is used for tea
Young leaves are used as vegetables or side dishes
The fruit is used to make wine
It is dried and used as a medicinal herb for longevity

Nothing to throw away
Matrimony vine
Strong spirit of service and sacrifice

In love together
I want to live!

포포나무

봄이 오면
산간벽지에
4~5m의 키를 자랑하는
포포나무 꽃봉오리
짓궂게 피어오르고

초야 곳곳에서
잘 자라는
포포나무꽃과 열매

열을 내리고
소변을 잘 보게 하며
혈압을 낮추는 데에
효과가 있고

바나나 향기에
망고 맛이 나는 포포나무 열매
단백질 함량이 높다

한방에서 소화불량
피부미용으로 쓰이네!

Popo Tree

When spring comes
In a mountainous area
Boasting a height of 4~5m
Poplar flower buds
Blooming mischievously

All over the wilderness
Vigorous
Poplar flowers and fruit

Bring down the fever
Make sure to urinate well
To lower blood pressure
It works

With the scent of bananas
Mango-flavored pawpaw fruit
High in protein content

Indigestion in Oriental Medicine
It's used for skin care!

아그배나무

꽃은 사랑이다

아그배나무
하얀 꽃은 온화하고 아름다워

떡 해 먹고
잼도 만들고
해독 작용이 있어
중독을 예방하는데
쓰인다

붉은색 예쁜 열매는
시고 떫어

소화불량을 치료하는 약재로
쓰인다.

Agabae Tree

Flowers are love

Agabae tree
White flowers are gentle and beautiful

Eat rice cakes
And make jam too
It has a detoxifying effect
To prevent addiction
It is used

The pretty red fruit
It's sour and bitter

As a medicinal herb to treat indigestion
It is used.

대추나무

울타리나
밭 언저리에 있는 대추나무
어느새 잎이 무성하고
키는 작아도
열매 열렸네!

천둥 번개로부터
농작물을 보호하고
키 크고 가시 많아
주변을 경계한다

가꾸지 않아도
많이 열리는 대추 열매
음식에 보약으로 쓰이고
다산에 다복을 가져온다

재질 또한 단단하여
도장과 불상, 나무못으로
사용되는 대추나무

우리네 살림살이와
연민의 정으로
엉켜있네!

Jujube Tree

A fence or
A jujube tree at the edge of a field
Before we knew it, the leaves were lush
Even though I'm short
The fruit has ripened!

From thunder and lightning
Protect your crops
Tall and thorny
Be wary of your surroundings

Even if you don't take care of it
Jujube fruit that grows abundantly
It is used as a health supplement in food.
Brings happiness to Dasan

The material is also strong
With a seal, a Buddhist statue, and wooden nails
Jujube tree used

Our life and
With compassion
It's tangled!

숲속의 나무들

제4부

안개나무

허전함 속에 고개 숙이고
꿈과 환상을 그리며
차곡차곡 쌓이는 단풍
바라보며 쓸쓸히 걷는다.

수양버들

수양버들이
축축 늘어진 연못가
아지랑이 하늘하늘

사방 연못에는 봄의 물결이
찰랑찰랑

연당(蓮堂) 주변에
나들이 나온 상춘객들
연지(蓮池)에 비친 수양버들 사이로
얼굴이 어른어른

늘어진 버들가지에
흐르는 초록 물결은
세월 따라
임을 기다리게 하네!

Weeping Willow

Weeping willow
A damp, sagging pond
Ajirangi sky sky

There are spring waves in the pond on all sides
Jjang jjang

Around Yeondang
Spring outing visitors
Between the weeping willows reflected in the lotus pond
Face is mature

On the drooping willow branches
The flowing green waves
As time goes by
You're keeping me waiting!

자귀나무

4~10m의 키로 자라고
해가 질 무렵에
우산 모양으로
활짝 피는 꽃

낮에는 펼치고
밤에는 오므라드는 이파리

나무 모양이 풍성하여
향긋한 꽃향기가
머리를 맑게 하고

가슴 두근거림을
치료해 주는 수피(樹皮)

꽃송이 모양이
공작새 깃털 같아

부부 금실의 상징
볼수록 신기한
환희의 자귀나무!

Acacia Tree

It grows to a height of 4 to 10 m.
At sunset
In the shape of an umbrella
A flower in full bloom

Spread out during the day
The leaves that sway at night

The tree shape is rich
The fragrant scent of flowers
Clear your head

My heart is pounding
Healing bark

The shape of a flower bud
Like a peacock's feather

Symbol of a couple's golden heart
The more I look at it, the more amazing it is
The tree of joy!

은행나무

산천초목 여기저기
길마다 왕자로 군림하는 은행나무
은행잎 하나로 임금 노릇하네

한여름
그 열정과 사랑으로
풍성하던 정겨움의 정취
가득 안겨주고

가을 향기 물씬 풍겨 와
화려했던 추억만큼
가랑잎 굴러다니는 소리
가을을 그립게 하네

아스팔트 위의 은행 나뭇잎
보석이 박혀 있는 듯
연모의 정으로 스치듯 밟는다

순간순간 샛노랗게 변하여
떨어지는 황금빛 은행잎
희망과 장수의 상징으로
누군가의 마음을 따뜻하게 하네!

Ginkgo Tree

Mountains, rivers, and plants here and there
The ginkgo tree that reigns like a prince on every road
One ginkgo leaf can act as king

Midsummer
With that passion and love
The sentiment of abundant affection
Give me full hugs

The scent of autumn is in the air
As splendid as the memories
The sound of falling leaves
It makes me miss fall

Bank leaves on asphalt
Looks like it's encrusted with jewels
Step on it with a feeling of affection

It turns bright yellow from moment to moment
Falling golden ginkgo leaves
As a symbol of hope and longevity
It warms someone's heart!

안개나무

연한 자주색 꽃잎
흩날리어

집으로 갈까!
누구랑 차를 마실까!
망설이다가

부스럭부스럭
낙엽 밟으며
이 골목 저 거리
사람들의 쾌활한 모습

누군가 다가와
아는 척하는 이 없어

허전함 속에
고개 숙이고
꿈과 환상을 그리며

길 위에 노랗게
차곡차곡 쌓이는 단풍
바라보며
쓸쓸히 걷는다.

Fog Tree

Light purple petals
Scattered

Let's go home!
Who should I drink tea with?
After hesitating

Rustle rustle
Stepping on fallen leaves
This alley, that street
The cheerful faces of people

Someone came
No one pretends to know

In the midst of emptiness
Bow your head
Drawing dreams and fantasies

Yellow on the road
Autumn leaves piled up one by one
Looking at
Walking alone.

치자나무

초여름이 되면
개울가 언덕 위에
치자나무꽃이 하얗게
고개를 내밀고 웃는다

한여름 무더위에
광택이 나는 이파리 사이로 핀
탐스러운 꽃송이들
여름을 반긴다

세상을 보려는 듯
산들바람에 향기를 흩날리며
활짝 핀 치자꽃
은은하게 별처럼 반짝이네

무더위 이겨내고
단풍이 흩날리면
이뇨제로 쓰이는
주황빛 열매가
주렁주렁.

Gardenia Tree

When early summer comes
On the hill by the stream
The flowers of the gardenia tree are white
Stick your head out and smile

In the midsummer heat
Pinned between glossy leaves
Lovely flower buds
Welcome summer

As if trying to see the world
Spreading its fragrance in the breeze
Full bloomed gardenia
Twinkling softly like a star

Beat the heat
When the autumn leaves fall
Used as a diuretic
Orange fruit
Dangling.

체리나무

화사한 봄 날씨에
솜처럼 하얗게
핀 꽃을 쳐다보니

꽃잎 사이로
초록 잎이 돋아나며
조화를 이룬다

분홍빛 체리 꽃송이
송이송이 매달려
한여름 무더위에
가지 엮으며 친구 만들고

고고하고 화려함을
가슴에 안은 채
저녁노을을 바라보며
꽃길을 가련다.

Cherry Tree

In the bright spring weather
White as cotton
Looking at the pin flower

Between the petals
Green leaves are sprouting
Harmonize

Pink cherry blossoms
Hanging one by one
In the midsummer heat
Making friends by weaving branches

Sophisticated and splendid
Holding you in my arms
Looking at the sunset
I wish you a path of flowers.

감귤나무

아름다운 제주도
와, 야자수다
하얀 감귤꽃이 참으로 예쁘다

천혜의 향기
노랗게 달린 감귤
정말 아름답구나

그대는 내게로 와서
뼈가 되고 살이 되고
생각이 되고 운명이 된다

인간을 위해 포장되어
배 타고 차 타고
식탁으로 보내어지는
감귤의 일생이 비감스럽다

Citrus Tree

Beautiful Jeju Island
Wow, it's a palm tree.
The white tangerine blossoms are really pretty.

The fragrance of nature
Yellow-colored tangerines
It's really beautiful

You come to me
Become bones and flesh
Become a thought and become destiny

Packaged for humans
By boat and by car
Sent to the table
The life of a tangerine is sad.

야자수나무

저 멀리
홀로 서 있는 야자수
외롭지 않은가!

거리마다
군락을 이루고
힘차게 서 있는 야자수

비바람이 스쳐도
탓하지 않고
세상을 관찰하는 야자수

봄이면
힘차게 새순이 솟아오르고
여름에는
무성한 녹음으로
가을에는 단풍으로
겨울에는 옷을 벗은 채
세월을 다시 돌아본다.

Palm Tree

Over there
A palm tree standing alone
Aren't you lonely!

On every street
Forming a colony
Palm trees standing strong

Even if the wind and rain pass by
Without blaming
Palm tree observing the world

In spring
New shoots are sprouting vigorously
In the summer
With lush greenery
In autumn, with maple leaves
In winter, without clothes
Looking back on the years.

골담초나무

파란 하늘
해맑은 들녘의 아침
살짝이 찾아드는 봄

노랗게
피어나는 수줍은 미소
아련한 골담초꽃의 향연

아, 봄의 유혹인가!
산야는 푸르고
일렁이는 초록 물결 사이로
골담초꽃의 밀어

대롱대롱
앙증스럽게 매달려

골담초 나무마다 넘실거리는
골담초꽃의 연가.

Corduroy Tree

Blue sky
A bright morning in the fields
Spring is coming in a flash

Yellow
A shy smile blooms
A feast of faint dandelion flowers

Ah, the temptation of spring!
The mountains and fields are green
Among the rippling green waves
The push of the dandelion flower

Dangling dangling
Hanging cutely

Every single tree is overflowing with dandelions
The love song of the dandelion.

편백나무

40m의 키
한국과 일본이 서식지

목질이 좋고
향이 뛰어나
실용성이 높다

풍부한 피톤치드로
아토피 치료에
효과 있고

가구용 목재는
니스 칠 없이
원목 그대로 쓴다.

Cypress Tree

40m tall
Korean and Japanese Habitat

The wood is good
The scent is excellent
Highly practical

With rich phytoncides
For the treatment of atopic dermatitis
It's effective

Wood for furniture
Without varnish
Use raw wood.

숲속의 나무들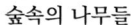

제5부

올리브나무

햇빛을 좋아하는 올리브나무
그 작고 하얀 꽃이 무리 지어 피는데

대나무

기름진 대나무 숲에서
하루에 90cm까지
자라는 대나무

더 많은 빛을
받기 위해
치열한 경쟁을 벌인다

빨리 자라기 위해
속을 텅텅 비운다

대나무의 성장 속도
세계에서
가장 빠른 식물 중 하나

100년에
한번 피는 대나무꽃

일생에
한번 보기 힘든
전설의 꽃.

Mamboo Tree

In the oily bamboo forest
Up to 90cm per day
Growing bamboo

More light
To receive
There is fierce competition

To grow up quickly
Empty your stomach

Bamboo growth rate
In the world
One of the fastest plants

In 100 years
Bamboo flower that blooms once

In a lifetime
It's hard to see once
The legendary flower.

올리브나무

햇빛을 좋아하는
올리브나무

과습에 약하여
배수가 잘되는 흙에서
잘 자란다

8~15m의 키를
자랑하는

그 작고 하얀 꽃이
무리 지어 피는데

지중해에 많이
분포한다.

Olive Tree

Sun-loving
Olive tree

Vulnerable to over-hydration
In well-drained soil
Grow well

The height of 8 to 15 meters
Bragging

The little white flower
They bloom in groups

In the Mediterranean Sea
It is distributed.

단풍나무

붉게 핀 가을 단풍
바람결에 흩날리는
낙엽 밟으며
낭만을 줍는다

갖가지 빛깔의 고운 단풍
서늘한 바람에 쓸리어
어찌할 줄 모르는
내 마음 같아
쓸쓸함은 더 깊어지네!

청명한 가을 하늘
맑은 계곡물
암벽과 단풍이 선명하게
조화를 이루어
천하의 절경
가을 내내 드리워져 있네!

단풍이 어울린 숲의 정취
매혹적이고
매우 아름다워
서럽도록
추억이 그리워지네!

Maple Tree

Red autumn foliage
Flying in the wind
Stepping on the fallen leaves
Pick up romance

Fine autumn leaves of various colors
I'm swept away by the cool wind
At a loss as to what to do
It's like how I feel
The loneliness gets deeper!

A clear autumn sky
Clear valley water
The rock walls and autumn leaves are clear
In harmony
A magnificent view of the world
It's been hanging over the fall!

The mood of a forest in autumn leaves
It's fascinating
It's very beautiful
Sadly
I miss the memories!

산수유나무

산수유
아직은 이른 봄
눈발 맞는 꽃봉오리

메마른 가지 위에
새 세상 열려오는가!

개울가
저 산야에
봄이 오는 소리

석조(石棗) 홍옥(紅玉) 그리는
바쁜 마음에
노란 네 잎의 꽃을 피운다.

A Cornelian Tree

Cornus
Early spring yet
A bud hit by snow

On a dry eggplant
Is the new world opening up!

By a stream
In the hills and fields
Sound that spring is coming

Drawing stone and red jade
Out of one's busy schedule
It blooms with four yellow leaves.

국수나무

가느다란 가지에서 피는
노란빛 꽃들이 어우러져
향기를 흩날리며
2.5m까지 자라는
국수나무

불그레한 줄기를
늘어뜨리며

탑처럼 생긴 꽃차례를
떠받드는 풍성한 이파리
나비처럼 날아갈 듯

여름이 되니
산천초목은
산새들의 놀이터가 되고
꽃과 별들의 장터가 된다

가시덩굴 같은 가지는
울타리로 쓰이고
복부비만 치료에도 효능이 있어
국수나무 차로 하루 한 잔씩!

Noodle Tree

Blooming on slender branches
Yellow flowers blend together
Spreading fragrance
Grows up to 2.5m
Noodle tree

The reddish stem
Hanging down

A tower-shaped inflorescence
Rich leaves that support
I feel like flying like a butterfly

It's summer
Mountains, rivers, and plants
Become a playground for mountain birds
It becomes a market of flowers and stars.

Branches like thorns
Used as a fence
It is also effective in treating abdominal obesity.
One cup of noodle tree tea a day!

선비나무

파란 하늘에
떠다니는 뭉게구름

한여름 무더위 속에
드물게 보이는 선비나무
어느 사이에
지천으로 널려

지역마다 여기저기
산천초목을 붉게
물들이고 있다

온통 초록 세상에
불그스름한 선비나무꽃이
한층 더 눈에 띈다

백일을 피워내어 백일홍 나무
잘 웃는다고 간지럼 나무
한여름의 청순한 화신이여!

Scholar Tree

In the blue sky
Floating cumulus cloud

In the midsummer heat
A rare sight of the zelkova tree
In the meantime
Spread all over the place

Here and there in each region
Turn the mountains and rivers red
Dyeing

All green in the world
The reddish-brown flowers of the magnolia tree
It stands out even more

The rose of Sharon tree blooms for a hundred days
Tickle tree that laughs a lot
Oh, the pure embodiment of midsummer!

동백나무

긴긴 매서운 겨울 지나며

붉고 시린 눈물을 지닌
남해의 겨울 동백꽃이
청청하고 싱그러운 생명력을
토해내듯 붉디붉게 피어나네!

청춘이 아쉬운 듯
그윽한 향기와 고결한 자태로
온 산과 바다에 영혼을 흩뿌리고
온종일 정열을 불사르네!

세월은 흘러
벌 나비 새들은
추억으로 사라지고

몰골 흉한 꽃송이
하소연 한 마디 못하고
대지의 품으로 곤두박질
최후를 맞는 꽃들의 널브러짐

전설을 아련히 가슴에 묻고
다소곳이 엎어져
바람이 스쳐 지나가네!

Camellia

After a long, bitter winter

With red and bitter tears
Winter camellia flowers in the South Sea
Fresh and refreshing vitality
It blooms bright red as if it's being vomited out!

It seems like I miss my youth
With a deep fragrance and noble appearance
Scatter your soul across the mountains and seas
Burning passion all day long!

Time goes by
Bees, butterflies, birds
Fading into a memory

Ugly flower bud
I can't even say a word of complaint
Plunge into the bosom of the earth
The fall of flowers that are about to end

I keep the legend faintly in my heart
Lie down quietly
The wind is blowing by!

모감주나무

8~10m의 키를 자랑하는
모감주나무

초록색 잎을 배경으로
노란색 꽃을 환하게 피워
쉽게 눈에 들어온다

꽃잎 떨어지는 모습이
황금비가 내리는 듯하다

모감주나무는
염주를 만드는
최고의 재료

가지마다
열매 주머니가 주렁주렁
매달려 있어

서로
인사를 하는 듯.

Motherwort

Boasting a height of 8~10m
Motherwort

With green leaves as a background
Blooming bright yellow flowers
Easy to see

The sight of petals falling
It looks like golden rain is falling

The zelkova tree
Making a prayer bead
Best ingredients

On each branch
Fruit bags hanging in bunches
Hanging on

Each other
As if saying hello.

자카란다 나무

보랏빛 색상으로 피는
여기 아름답고 인기 있는
자카란다 꽃송이에
빗물이 맺혔네!

보랏빛 눈물방울
낙화를 재촉하고

대지에 내려앉은
청잣빛 우아함이
불타는 가슴을 보여주는 듯
사랑을 고백하네!

자카란다 꽃길을
걸어가면

목마른 내 마음이
불길처럼 타올라

한줄기의 힘찬
그리움으로!

Jacaranda Tree

Blooming in purple color
Here are some beautiful and popular
In the jacaranda flower buds
It's raining!

Purple teardrops
Urging the flowers to fall

Settled on the ground
Blue elegance
It seems to show a burning heart
I confess my love!

Jacaranda flower path
If you walk

My thirsty heart
Burn like a flame

A single powerful line
With longing!

후박나무

울릉도에서 자라는
후박나무 묘목
한번 심어 놓으면
그늘이나 메마른 땅에서도
잘 자라

비가 오지 않아도
찌푸리지 않고
눈이 많이 내려도
절대로 탓하지 않는다

차라리 시들어 죽을지라도

꽃이 피고
열매가 맺고
뿌리가 튼튼해지면
가로수나
생울타리로 이용한다

온갖 질병
한약재로 다스리며
500살 수령이 다할 때까지
후박나무는 그 진한 향기를
잃지 않는다.

Mackerel

Growing up in Ulleungdo
Mackerel seedlings
Once you plant it
Even in the shade or on dry ground
Grow up well

Even if it doesn't rain
Without frowning
Even if it snows a lot
I never blame you

I'd rather wither and die

Flowers are blooming
It bears fruit
When the roots become strong
Street trees
Used as a hedge

All kinds of diseases
Treated with herbal medicine
Until the age of 500 is reached
The cinnamon tree has a strong fragrance
Don't lose.

숲속의 나무들

초판인쇄 2025년 7월 25일 초판발행 2025년 7월 30일

지은이 장현경
펴낸이 장현경 펴낸곳 엘리트출판사
편집 디자인 마영임
등록일 2013년 2월 22일 제2013-10호

서울특별시 광진구 긴고랑로15길 11 (중곡동)
전화 010-5338-7925
E-mail : wedgus@daum.net

정가 14,000원

ISBN 979-11-87573-51-7 03810